Welcome, athlete!

POWER LIFTING COLORING BOOK

Reconnect with your strength by coloring high quality original art featuring powerlifters, weightlifters, strongman/strongwoman, gymnasts, bodybuilding and crossfit heroes and heroines.

Laugh at gym stereotypes! Find the fitness bikini chick, the Instagram guy, the bro lifter, the bench press gymnast with a huge arch, the long-armed deadlifter, and the buff dad lifting with his daughter.

Your review on Amazon, Google, or another platform through which you purchased this book would help our small artists collective!

© 2022 Truecoloringbook.com. All rights have been reserved
ISBN: 979-8-9869829-0-8

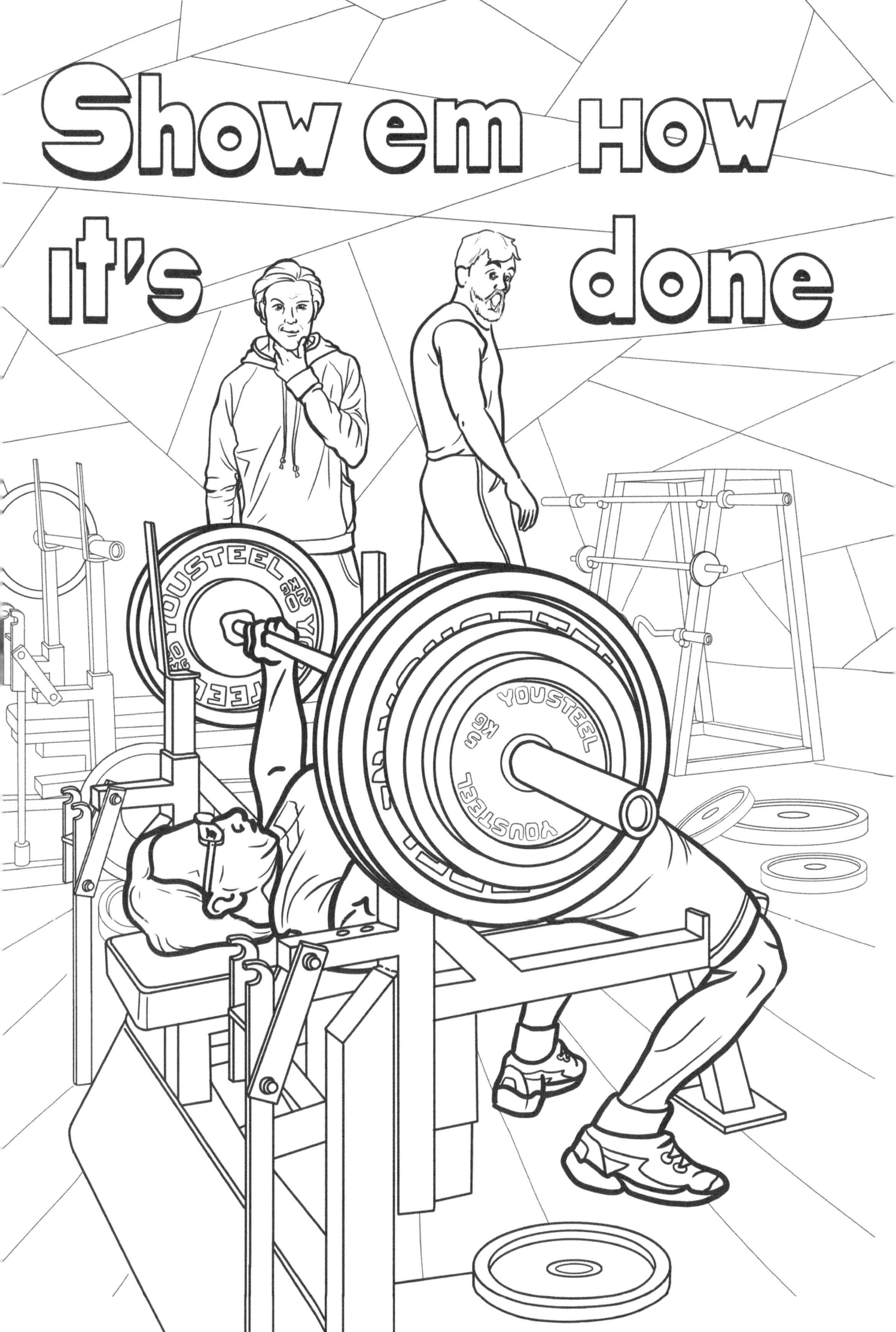

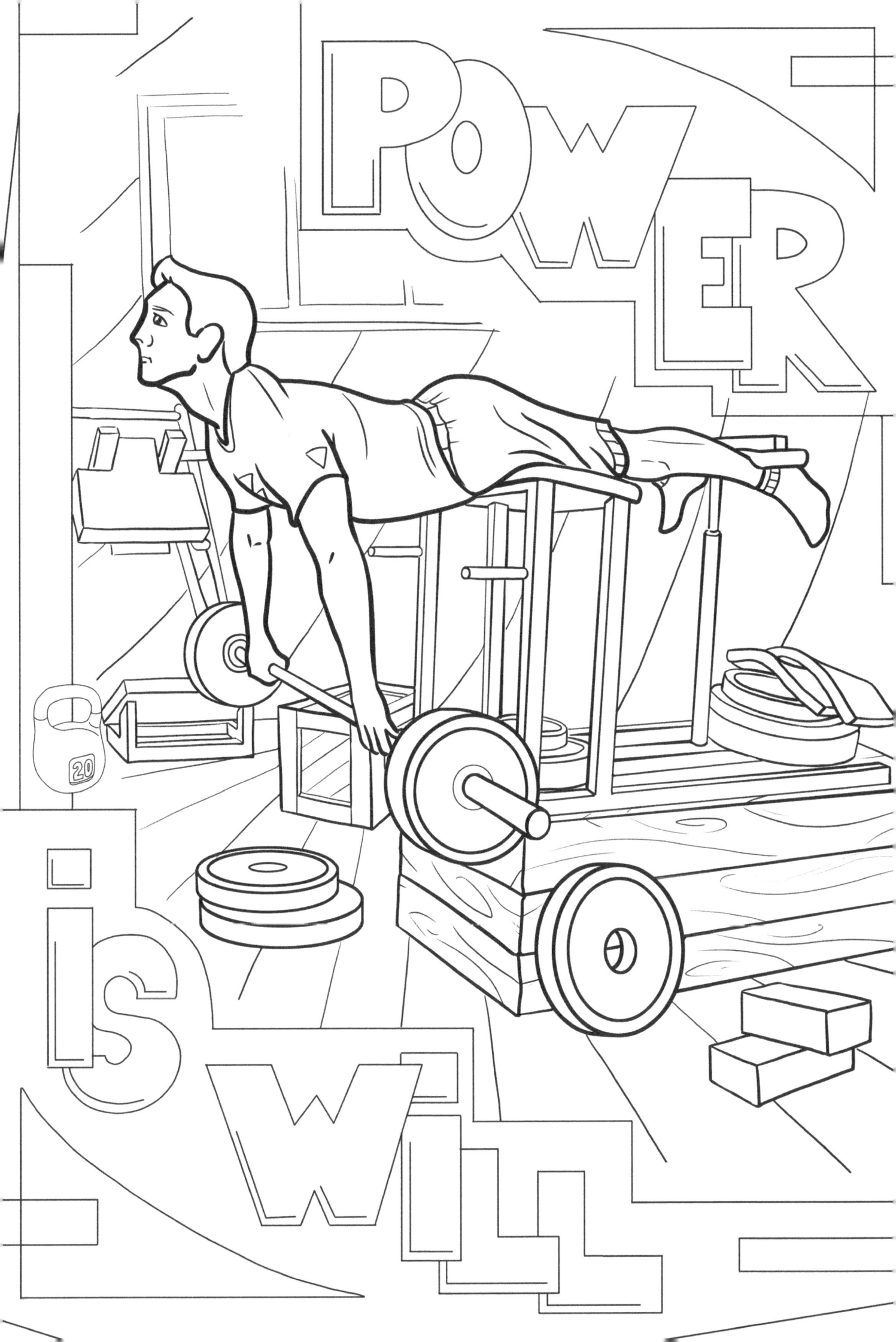